IDEAL HOME

a detached look at modern living

photographs by

JOHN R J TAYLOR

Introduction by Mark Haworth-Booth

Text by Charles Newton

CORNERHOUSE
PUBLICATIONS

Mark Haworth-Booth is the Curator of Photography at the Victoria & Albert Museum in London. He is well known for his writings on photography and photographers and has instigated and curated numerous successful photographic exhibitions at the V & A. He is committed to building a comprehensive collection of British and International photography at the Museum.

Charles Newton is a Curator in the Department of Design, Prints and Drawings at the Victoria & Albert Museum. He is the author and co-author of books and exhibition catalogues relating to Art and Design and is responsible for integrating the Searight collection of pictures of the Middle East into the collection of the V & A. Presently he is preparing an exhibition entitled 'HOUSEHOLD CHOICES' which will examine the role of consumers and entrepreneurs in the continuum of design.

John R J Taylor would like to thank Brenda and Nicky for their co-operation, and understanding, and Hertfordshire College of Art and Design, St Albans for their support.

The first photograph by John R J Taylor I ever saw was his picture of an English Sunday afternoon (*North London, 1982* – reproduced on back cover). It won Taylor a prize in a London-wide competition and the Victoria & Albert Museum bought a print of it from him while he was still a student at the Royal College of Art. The picture was later used in an issue of *Creative Camera* on 'The Home Front' (October 1982) and more recently made an appearance in the American magazine *Aperture* in their issue 'British Photography: Towards a Bigger Picture' (Fall, 1988). I remember showing this photograph to my colleague Charles Newton about five years ago. He recognized the particular north London suburb without hesitation. Any British viewer will instantly recognize the time – Sunday afternoon – if not necessarily the place. After lunch, the stillness not really broken by the buzz of an electric mower. The child (or children) put down for a nap – one takes in the soft toy on the garden table at once – time for a look at the paper. A local paper by the looks of it – you can just read the words MAIL and the headline QUEEN COURAGE, or QUEEN'S COURAGE. The assassination attempt at Trooping the Colour, perhaps? Or the bedroom intruder at Buckingham Palace? Such events become part of the chronology of our world, along with the paraphernalia of investitures, jubilees, royal weddings, royal funerals. Ordinary life goes on and goes on being ordinary…and unrepeatable and unique. This picture shows Taylor's clear ability as a decisive moment photographer, despite its perfectly placid subject: the moment was selected with dramatic and geometrical precision. It is worth mentioning this, because Taylor has chosen a quite different way of photographing for this series.

He moved inside the house with his viewpoint, photographing with the impunity of a blood relation. He snoops around the house on behalf of an idea and a posterity. There is a famous photo essay which records one day in the life of an ordinary Russian working family in 1931. Taylor's photographs record the ordinary too. Do they do more than that? First of all, they make one put quotation marks around the word 'ordinary'. Without melodrama, the photographs insist on the importance of their subjects. Taken together, the photographs become absorbing. This is one of the few albums of photographs that one wishes did not come to an end. And, actually, the series continues in one's own imagination: instead of touring the domesticity of strangers one begins to ponder one's own habitat. The camera represents the scrutiny of a stranger, in any case, but this series brings that feature into the foreground. So we continue Taylor's series in our own homes but with something of the frankness of camera vision. Charles Newton's essay eloquently describes the experience of looking at these photographs.

What of their antecedents? From the 1850's photography has been, in Lady Eastlake's memorable formulation, 'a household word and a household want, used alike by love, business and justice'. Unfortunately, it was rather seldom applied to the task of recording households – the people in them, yes; the objects in them, no. The first director of the Victoria and Albert Museum, Sir Henry Cole, was a rare exception. As an amateur, he photographed his living room and bedroom in 1856. There is a remarkable photograph from about the same date by another amateur, Henry Pollock, who recorded the remains of an elaborate lunch. I can think of no other photograph of dirty plates in the 19th century – just to put the matter baldly! John Taylor's work has definite contemporary precedents, however: his choice of unusual viewpoints and subjects is reminiscent of the colour photography of William Eggleston. The idea of a catalogue of suburban lifestyle is much associated with Bill Owens. Taylor admires Bill Owen's *Suburbia* (San Francisco, 1973). Another of Taylor's enthusiasms is Lewis Baltz, a Californian who has made bleak exquisite photographic inventories of American housing developments. These are closer to Taylor because of their mission of cataloguing the uncatalogued.

He shares with Owens a desire to record 'ordinary' lives and he is like all three American photographers I have named in clearly being curious about how things look in photographic form. Cognate photographers of interiors are another American, Catherine Wagner, and the Canadian, Lynne Cohen.

I am reminded of a remark by Ralph Waldo Emerson: 'We eat and drink and wear perjury and fraud in a hundred commodities'. I do not think this work is in any sense a denunciation of materialism or of such commodities as are displayed. However, I do think the photographs underline the role of these commodities in common life. The design historian Stephen Bayley exaggerates when he describes material culture as, in effect, the true culture of the 20th century – but he exaggerates engagingly. The commodities here have their secret histories, and their public histories may well include perjury and fraud (is there any alleged Guinness in the house?) – but they also represent inspiration and invention. Am I serious? Well, have you ever

shampooed a child's hair? You can't look at the photograph of the bathroom, which includes that invaluable new product (a light, fibre halo) which keeps soapy water out of a child's eyes, without feeling gratitude to an unknown inventor. It was not until I saw the photograph that I realized how grateful I am. Taylor's photographs work like that.

Belatedly, an urgent awareness of the consequences of our habitual lifestyles is going to cause reappraisal of many features of ordinary life as never before. This is a very timely photographic project.

Mark Haworth-Booth

The Ancient Chinese spoke of the multiplicity of the world as the *Ten Thousand Things*. The sheer number of everyday objects, concepts, natural phenomena, human desires, in short all the innumerable details of life were regarded as a distraction in the way of understanding. They were the individual trees that prevented you from seeing the wood as a whole. Confronted by a vast sea of things pleading for attention, it is no wonder that a mortal is tempted to give up and concentrate only on what is generally believed to be significant.

Human beings, although fitted with massive brains, are paradoxically also equipped with efficient mental filters which limit their use and prevent the mind from being overwhelmed by the sheer quantity of information that floods in from our senses at every moment of waking life. Most of the time we have no choice in the matter. We literally have no time to stand and stare, if only for reasons of self-preservation. The result is that now people never look with more than a cursory glance at anything that is perceived to be ordinary. As for the stage beyond mere recognition, human interest and attention is usually focussed on what is claimed to be extraordinary, the rare, the unusual.

The strategy that we normally employ to cope with the world is to ignore most of it, and concentrate on a narrow selection commonly supposed to be important which makes the strongest impact on the senses. In the hurly-burly of everyday life, this is the obvious thing to do. However, if this strategy is transferred to art, and particularly to photography, it often proves to be a blind alley, because it is subject to the law of diminishing returns. The progressive striving after recording or setting-up ever more significant or sensational moments creates emotional inflation, until the spectator, and sometimes even the photographer, is numbed or turns away in disgust.

However, there is another, more difficult strategy. Everything is potentially loaded with meaning, if only now and then we took the time to look in a different way. What is needed, now and then, is that which encourages us to realize that ordinary things, even the banal, are potentially extraordinary and imbued with meaning on all levels, and that this meaning is limited only by the narrowness of our existing knowledge or imagination.

It is said that a few medieval alchemists did *not* believe (contrary to popular opinion) that the Philosophers Stone was located in exotic lands and guarded by dragons, although it was believed to hold the secret of the universe and transmute base metal into gold. The subtle alchemists claimed that this was merely the 'gold of the vulgar', and *their* Stone was so common and yet unnoticed that it could lie in the street ignored by virtually everyone. In other words, the secret was in everyday things and very close, which concealed it all the more.

At first sight anything less like a medieval alchemist than John Taylor, photographer, is difficult to imagine. He is saying, quietly with the alchemists, that understanding lies in the house or in the street, unseen and neglected except by those that have eyes to see. Despised or unnoticed by the many, it is yet within their scope if they do but look.

In his photographs John Taylor makes us stop and think, or rather, in his diffident way, invites us to do so. We are not badgered, manipulated, nudged knowingly by pictures of significant moments, nor by plangent images of disaster and high and obvious emotion. It is a rare invitation to reconsider what was normally taken for granted and think again about what all of it means, and why, particularly, it looks like it does.

For example, you can read the personality of people from the things that are in their houses, just as much as you can analyse and speculate about how everything came to look as it does. From the photograph of a new pair of sensible children's shoes, just taken out of the box, or of a house plant against a skirting board, there is a whole textbook of sociology to be written, and read, but if you can read the photograph, it is not necessary.

There used to be a hierarchy of images, so that there were things considered to be worthy (or unworthy) of being photographed. Yet objects gain a new aura merely because they are selected and isolated, and looked at again with new eyes. The act of choosing to focus attention on them changes what they are, or how you perceive them, which may be the same thing.

John Taylor delights in his sister's house, a north London suburban semi, a type of house which is to many people the epitome of ordinariness. To him (and to me) it is subtly revealed as a potential stage for every kind of event, mystery, romance, stress, good and bad feeling. Again and again in John Taylor's photographs you are invited to speculate on and interpret events and attitudes beyond the picture.

Many houses in Britain resemble this interior, but it is an error to assume that they and their inhabitants are all the same. This mistake comes from the unintelligent application of broad sociological theory and not from specific observation. Statistical charts are very useful in their place, but do not actually tell you what any individual thing is like. Although it was not John Taylor's primary intention, this sequence of photographs will prove a valuable documentary record which will eventually have historical value.

Fashion changes so rapidly that many things in these photographs have already been superseded and swept away. That is the paradox: what was once mistakenly assumed to be so ordinary as to be not worthy of notice, frequently becomes part of the rarest category of ephemera in Museums. John Taylor is asking us, I believe, to stop and think about the ordinary world around us. The superb technical quality of his photography enables us to see without distortion what is there, as if through our own eyes newly opened.

Charles Newton

THE PHOTOGRAPHS

The captions to the photographs are very brief extracts from a two-hour tape-recording made on 6 March 1989 in the house where the photographs had been taken. Present were: Brenda; her husband, Nicky; her brother, John Taylor; her daughter Olivia; her sister-in-law, Katrina Taylor; and myself as interviewer.

Brenda was shown the photographs of her home destined for this book, and responded to questions about them. I decided to use small (but I hope, representative) fragments of her comments only, although all the other members of the family, particularly Nicky, contributed to the discussion.

I am very grateful to Brenda and Nicky, first for their generous hospitality, and secondly for tolerating my stream of questions.

C.N.

The Ideal Home series consists of approximately 60 images from which a selection was made for this book. All of the photographs were taken in one north London home between 1983 and 1987. The series is a constituent part of a larger body of work featuring north London suburbia and the edge of the green belt.

J.R.J.T.

We both liked that view, didn't we? There's a little bit of history... there was an old couple who lived there who were extremely friendly... and had a fabulous vegetable plot and we used to watch them, always busy... do you remember? They are both now deceased and that house was sold to my next door neighbour's oldest daughter. So everything there I feel comfortable about. Nicky often admires his work from this window after a hard day in the garden...

It's not just a light bulb...they're my favourite light bulbs. It's a very big bulb compared to the normal...I saw them displayed when I bought a light-fitting. The (wallpaper) patterns are out of a Linda Beard catalogue. She does very pretty female bedrooms...she now does mens as well. It coordinates with the bed linen.

The chair is from the dining room suite…I
told him basically what I wanted and it was
delivered. I looked at it and I realized it
wasn't my cup of tea but for the price I had
to keep it…because it was very reasonable.
I hate it when it's being decorated…I hate
being unorganized, but when I have the
time I enjoy decorating, myself, but I hate
to see the mess…I don't think that's an un-
common feeling, amongst women anyway.

The stickers ... that got her a severe telling-off, when that happened. It was done without my permission ... This was not allowed because at the time the room was still O.K., although it needs decorating now. It took a long hard time to remove them with no help from herself.

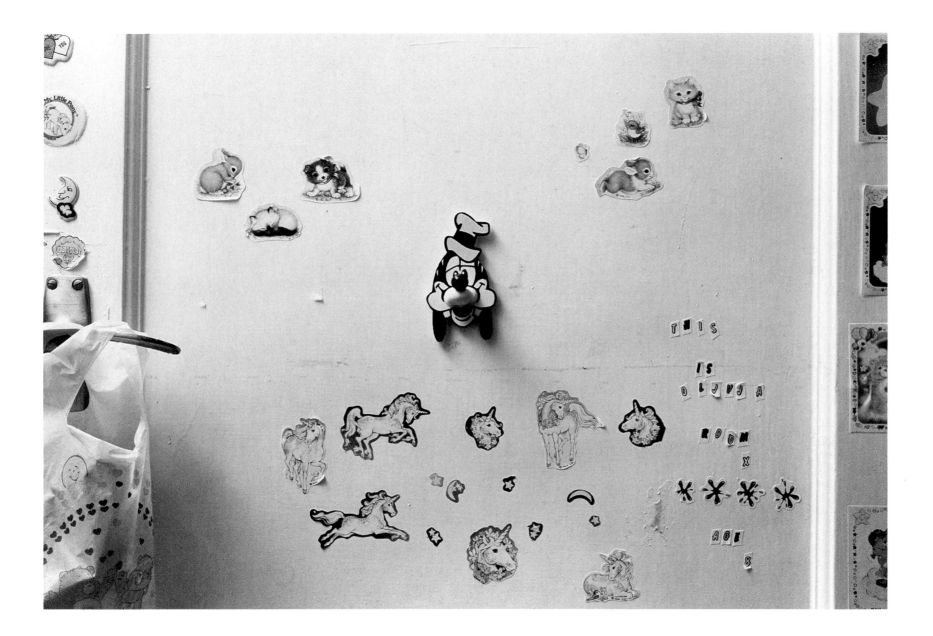

5   School uniform

That was her first one... that was at the
ready for the morning.

I've recently given those away: these shoes on the left, they're bright red. Those I bought for John and Katrina's wedding. I still like them. Those got ruined on a holiday, they were my aerobic shoes. I've still got this white bag which was made for me by a lady in Covent Garden...so when I was out and about with Olivia, everything was in the bag. There's nothing like putting a pair of new shoes on...it's a nice feeling...

I hate that picture. It's dark and dismal and my room isn't dark and dismal. It's a festoon, or an *Austrian*, blind. It was up for four years, but it became so incredibly dusty . . . and because of the design of them it couldn't really be washed. It was pretty but never a practical thing.

That's the type of shoe that the school insists on, they have got to have brown, they have got to have sensible, so it's always something like that. I have always told her to put her shoes together... even when they are ready to be polished they're not to be in a heap, they are to be together.

That hanging on the shower head was...
put around the hair line...so that the water
would not run into (Olivia's) eyes, and she
used that until she was about four or five.

The lime down here...when I first came to
England I could not believe the rubbish you
found around taps...I could never understand why it was happening...I realized it
was the hardness of the water which in
Scotland we just don't have.

I always have something like that up there. There's a table up there at the moment with something on it. I get fed up with seeing things in the same position...I just like change.

She always lies there . . . she likes the sunshine. I had all the glass replaced . . . it's much brighter now.

The armchairs…they're all gone. Oh my God, I hated them. My mother-in-law…I bought them…to keep her on the sweet side. That jug I loved and then my sister Barbara took it because it belonged to her… she wheeched it away the next time she came down…It's from my grandmother's house.

He did have another arm...I probably dropped him when I was washing him. He went really yellow...I don't know what it was made of. It was fairly smooth until I washed it and then it started to flake...and go sandy...His toenails were perfect.

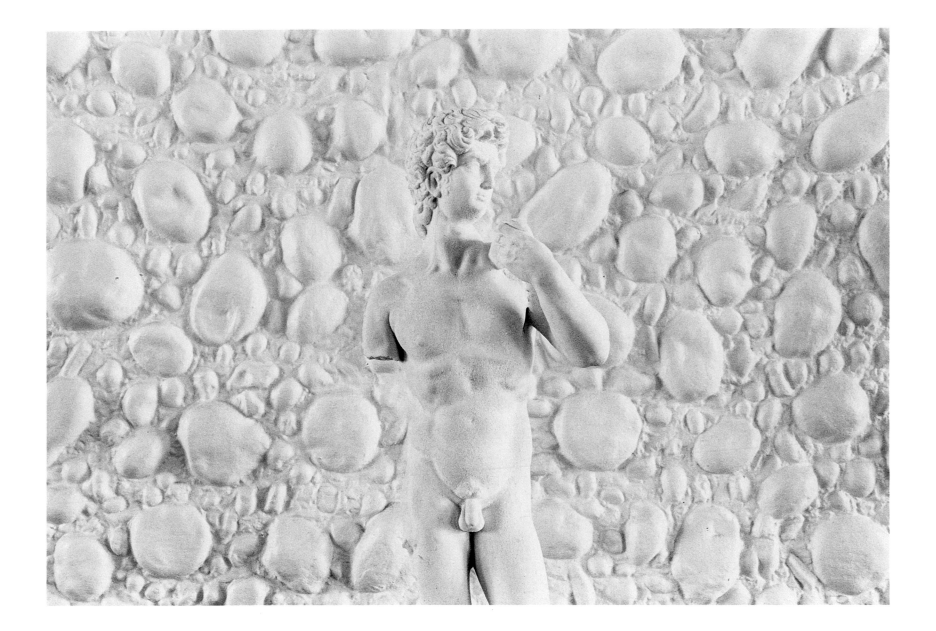

14   **Living room cabinet with coffee
set and wineglasses**

*I've still got all those, except half the glasses
are smashed. It stays like that … polished
clean and gleaming.*

At the time we were just trying to find a piano to go into that space there. That's why it looks so bare... The piano is not only a musical instrument it's a piece of furniture and you've got to buy the right piece of furniture, and bear in mind, it's got to be the right sound as well.

I've still got that lamp but the shade got so *thin...it got so used that the heat...it started to crack. We needed a nest of tables ...for cheap tables they have lasted.*

Still got the television, still got the video! I'd like a new flat screen TV but my practical husband says we don't need one, because there is nothing wrong with the one we've got. We bought it in Selfridges about a week after we got married because we had all the money pinned to us at our Greek wedding.

Copies again from down the market! I wished I had kept them because...the frames...I could have done my collage in. I think we were going to get some more and group them...

That picture is still on the board...that one *of Nicky and I and Olivia...all my photo-* *poppy from school and made a cross and*
graphs I keep...that was taken in Brent *pinned it on...and anything she makes at*
Cross shopping centre. Olivia had bought a *school stays pinned up for a while.*

They were just going out … illegal tender …
I started to save every pound note … I've
still got that jug … it moves about.

Well, John takes some funny shots... I'm kind of used to it... That's Cheddar with chives... it was probably old and mouldy and did not look appealing to me to cook with either. I'm afraid that that apple belonged to my daughter... I recognise... the baby teeth marks. She was then five or six. She didn't have a fierce appetite then ... That apple would never have happened today... that would have been devoured along with the cheese.

I must have done shopping that day. It looks fairly full... it doesn't last long. I try and shop, a big shop, once a week and buy bread and, perhaps, fruit midweek... I'm at work all day long and like to come home and it's there... Those are home grown tomatoes, by Nicky...

Marlboro...duty free...typical Nicky... I hate smoking and so they're always hidden in a cupboard. These are double eggcups which we got as a wedding present. Alka Seltzers and Andrews...well, that speaks for itself...

At the time I liked frogs...it seemed to be the phase. I hate real frogs but I like ceramic ones. Behind there is my make-up bag. It's in case I run out. I never go out anywhere without a bit of lipstick on. I'm a bit vain, I'm afraid.

Sparkle, Ajax, bleach...I still use all those products there...It's under the sink...

that's a big bottle of Comfort, I wonder why I got that...they don't do them that big now. I sometimes cut those labels off, if

I'm feeling canny. That was four litres of Comfort...it must have been from the cash and carry.

…Perfectly clean and shiny…yes…not changed since that picture…except I have lost one of these sharp knives, unfortunately. I think it got thrown away with the potato peelings. It's just what we bought when we first got married…and never replenished it …that's quite nice…

I've still got that cooker and it still looks gleaming like that. I had to have one that was self-cleaning. I have found a new method of cleaning those (shelves)...A tip from my sister Barbara who's cleaner round the house than I am.

I wanted a large glass fruit dish...I also make green salad and put it on there, or I used to use it as a cheese dish as well. We eat a lot of fruit and we both like to see a huge dishful.

I can't look at that, sorry. It's disgusting.

John's daft... I just don't understand his reasons sometimes. I just think John found it a joke and pinned it up on the college wall or something. I know it's natural and it has to be done every day but I am not the one to pick it up, I'm afraid.

I don't know what John saw there at all...
She'd just have been lying there, wondering
what the hell John was doing. That is her
normal pose in many pictures, actually
...The dog's house has been a bit changed
...it's got horseshoes pinned on it now...
still got the same hose except it's got shorter
through the years.

In the winter we stop her going down the garden because she makes mud tracks and ruins the lawn, so she's restricted. Olivia and I loved the rabbits, and Nicky chose the bird bath because he's always feeding the birds and watching them.

That was how we were going to build the

barbecue, and I didn't like it so near the house... There was too much going on... I wanted it quite clear.

This had newly been painted...unfortun-ately it does not look as fresh as that now. This glass was fairly new as well...one of the builders had been locked out one day and got in through this window...and cracked it, so he replaced it with the same glass as he had used inside.

That's Nicky's story…He must have been decorating as he has got two bottles of Ronson Gas to burn paint off with. I do like to see the garage with everything off the floor …Olivia uses the garage as a playroom in the summer…It's a shame, all that there, because when you are in the garage, these windows behind the shelf have got a lovely little view…over both gardens…(However) I prefer all that stuff out of the house…

Nothing's changed...she's still nice, the car. We had her since she was a year old...she's still in excellent condition. The daffodils...

We've been here 13 years...they were there when we came so I wouldn't like to imagine how old those bulbs are.

It...looks very tumble down, doesn't it, but there again, a lot happening as well. The original arbour had collapsed, so you took it all down and burnt it. We have another vine that grows along this fence...The neighbours love it so we slung half of it over to them...we both look after it either side. You just don't see much of the houses in the summer, because it's...very plentiful.